THE
SUNSHINE OF MY LIFE

THE SUNSHINE OF MY LIFE

By
Denzil Fairbairn

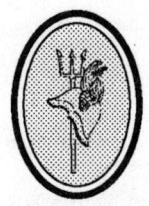

HERMES
2 Tavistock Chambers, Bloomsbury Way, London WC1A 2SE

First Published 1994

© Copyright by Denzil Fairbairn

This book is copyrighted under the Berne Convention. No portion may be reproduced by any process without the copyright holder's written permission except for the purposes of reviewing or criticism, as permitted under the Copyright Act of 1956.

ISBN 1 86032 020 1

Typesetting by Jim Barry

Cover illustration by Maria Neczyporczuk

Made and printed in Great Britain by Booksprint, Bristol, England

PREFACE

The Sunshine of my life, is the Golden Knowledge of Spirit, brought down through the Ether by a teacher from the fifth Sphere of thought, within the Spirit World. This teacher's Spirit name is *Sunshine* and when perambulating through this mortal coil, he was a priest of the Inca nation. At the time of this incarnation however, the Inca religion involved much ritual and as we all know, human sacrifice took place, and although the Inca nation were a truly proud race of people, upon reflection there wasn't really a great deal to be proud of in this practise. Therefore, as you can imagine, he had much to learn when passing from this physical world of ours. His religion must not be judged because his people believed it to be right, therefore, for them there was nothing wrong in what they were doing. It was right in a sense for they believed totally in an Afterlife and they believed in an ultimate power which was their God. It may well have had a different name to the one which we understand and was represented by the Sun but in essence it was still God.

You will find that *Sunshine* has learned much whilst in the spirit world and it is now being passed on to all those who have eyes to see and ears to listen.

INTRODUCTION

Many of you may have only recently discovered a belief in, or acceptance of life away from the physical body with which we are all burdened. Many of you may have been fortunate enough to have been aware and to have had a strong faith in the Spirit world for many years. Mine is, if you like, more of a rediscovery, a new understanding of this truth, which has been rekindled in me over the last few years or so.

I was brought up with the delights of having a father who was a trance medium. Although not a famous or even a particularly well known medium, except to the congregations of a small group of Spiritualist churches where he regularly took Sunday service, the work carried out through him, by Spirit, was indeed of the highest order. During the earlier years of my childhood, up until I reached the age of twelve or thirteen, it seemed that both my Father and Spirit were resting. A mutually accepted rest period which provided the opportunity for dad to have a family and a life without any disruption. My mother always said, however, that Spirit never really stopped their work. The quality of control and the deepness of trance, which was now apparent, was obviously a result of the development work which had continued to take place during fathers sleep state, through those quieter years. It was a wonderful experience to be brought up in those circumstances, I felt and deep down I knew that I was really too young then to take in, let alone appreciate, all the wonderful knowledge that Spirit was endeavouring to impart to my family. I needed no proof of life continuance because I was there in the middle of it all, I had proof every day. It was all so natural to me. I realise now that it was a blinkered acceptance, it was just like day and night, it was always there, therefore it must always have been so. Although I feel deeply honoured to have had such an upbringing, I have to confess that much of what was given to me by Spirit at that time just went in one ear and out of the other and was rarely given a second thought.

My father, George Fairbairn, was born in March 1920, into a family eventually totalling ten brothers and sisters. As you can probably imagine with such a large family there wasn't a great deal to go around, in fact like many families of that era they were materially very poor, but as a family they were very close and so gained in many other aspects. I would add, that upon reflection, from other books I have read that describe the early years of many of our more famous mediums, they nearly all seem to have had humble beginings. This must be the stamp of approval which helps to make them a more spiritual person and more likely to take up this sort of work.

Father was introduced into Spiritualism shortly after marrying his wife Joan, in 1947. Mother's family, which hailed from South Wales, already had a long tradition of communication and development work with the spirit world. In fact it was in this family circle that some ten years or so earlier, the conditions were right to enable the development of a renowned physical medium to take place, that of Jack Webber. He also married into my mother's family, he was perhaps a little better known than the many other trance mediums.

My Father reluctantly took part in these family circles to begin with, in the belief that he was sitting to help other members of the family in their development of mediumship. He didn't care so much for the "spooks" at first, but as his interest grew, so did his eagerness to learn as much about the spirit world as he could, from books and from as much personal experience as he could obtain. He would go to see other mediums of the day and soon he was to talk about nothing else because nothing else seemed to be as interesting to him. It wasn't to be too long before father's own mediumship was to commence in it's own right and I hasten to add, with not one iota of reluctance from him, just an open heart. Gradually controls were attracted to and attached themselves to him, and soon his band of guides had begun to form. They were all to play their own equally important parts in the variety of work which was to become my father's life. He was in the earlier period of his work, inspired to write poetry and prayers. These were fortunately preserved on scraps of paper and made into a book by his eldest daughter, as a birthday present. One of my favourites is a tribute to *'Guides And Helpers.'*

> We pray O God that Thou may Bless
> Those beautiful Souls of Tenderness
> That Come to us from time to time
> With words of comfort, Love divine.
> We ask they may be given Power
> To pattern their lives as a Spiritual Flower
> That they may fulfill their daily task
> Enlightening lonely Souls that ask.
> A special prayer we send to Thee
> For those who give their help so free
> Through them the seeds of love are sown
> Themselves their names, they make not known.
> We ask for them a devoted place
> A favoured corner within Thy Grace
> For all the work so freely given
> Admit them Lord into Thy Heaven.
> We close our prayer to Thee Sweet Lord
> And when parted from the Silver Cord
> Our one desire is to be as Good
> As the Guides and Helpers of the Brotherhood.

He was also inspired by spirit to draw portraits of his guides and helpers and of complete strangers, who were to become known to his family later on in life. Also bestowed upon him was the gift of healing. This was performed, whilst he was in a deep trance, by his doorkeeper and healer, *Mahanka*, a Blackfoot Indian who when on the earthplane was medicineman for his Tribe. *Mahanka* spoke with us on many occasions during family circles, giving us advice and passing on to us some of the knowledge that he had been given during seminars he had attended in the world of spirit. He became as loved by us all as a Grandfather would be. In fact he always refered to my mother as his little daughter and this was accepted to be the case from a previous incarnation when they were both on the earthplane together. Many wonderful results were achieved in this healing capacity, with the correction of slipped discs, misalignment of joints and trapped nerves, all producing instant or near instant relief for the patients. Manipulation was *Mahanka's* speciality, or so it seemed, with many a crooked man leaving our house after a healing session, completely upright and free from pain. It wasn't always conditions requiring manipulation that came to father for relief. On one special occasion, which I will carry with me for ever in my memory, was the vastly improved vision restored to a little girl who was classified as blind. She wasn't one hundred percent blind when she came to *Mahanka* for healing but her vision was restricted to being able to see shadows in strong sunlight. After several healing sessions her sight was improved so that she could now see colours and identify all that had once been just a gloomy blur. I first realised that a small miracle had occured, when she was waiting at the front gate of her house with her dad and she quite exitedly said to him, "Here comes mummy," who was some 40 - 50 yards away, walking along the road towards them. She went on to describe the colours and pattern on her mother's dress to her elated father. We were also very fortunate to have in my father's band of guides a nerve doctor, his name was *Tai-Ola* who was a Tibetan. He was always very calm and softly spoken which instantly seemed to put you at your ease when he visited. Fortunately, his services were rarely directly required, but I am sure he was always on hand to give advice or help *Mahanka* when the need arose and it was always lovely to have him come along and speak with us during home circles.

As my father's mediumship progressed we were able to have fairly regular home circles when many friends and loved-ones from the world of spirit would come to spend a little time with us, renewing old aquintances and introducing those who had passed but not fully realised the condition. We would talk to them and help them on their way and inevitably they would return at some stage to let us know how they were getting on. One gentleman who became quite a regular visitor to our circles was Will Urqhart. He was an American trapper from the last century who whilst out on the mountains had frozen to death. All he seemed to be worried about was finding his favourite sheep-skin coat that he had lost. It seemed this coat was his pride and joy and by his return visit he had managed to find it. We also had the great pleasure of meeting other members of my Father's Band of Guides, who were all by now well established. One who rarely spoke but who always made his presence felt with that all to familiar tingling feeling, like electricity running through you, was *Momba*, a Zulu warrior, and my father's power guide. He was actually the first of the band to speak to my father, this was accomplished by direct voice transmission during a physical circle he once attended. Another who visited our home circles was 'Dickie,' a London barrow-boy, who passed earlier this century with what he colourfully described as the dreaded lurgy, or as we would know it Tuberculosis. His trademark, which let everyone know that he was around, was to come through bringing a cold feeling with him, he would then rub his hands together vigorously in an effort to warm himself up. This invariably made all the sitters feel a cold sensation, even if only for the time that he was visiting us. He would then generally cajole everyone into singing a few songs, selected from his large repertoir of old 'Sally-Army' hymns, picked up and remembered from the times he used to follow that noble group of people around the streets of London.

Next would come *Nemani*, he was a 6 year old Sudanese boy, whose family had been slaves. He was a real character who always managed to put the sitters at their ease by explaining to them in his own words how he came to pass into spirit at such an early age. He was climbing a tree which had it's branches reaching out over a river. He fell from one of the branches into the river, he went down to the bottom, then he came up, he went down, then he came up, then he went down and then he came up. Then he got a fever and he was hot, then cold, then he got hot, then he got cold and then he passed into spirit, even though he didn't realise it at the time because he was so little. He doesn't want to get any older he says, and in the 25 years or so that I have known him, he has always been 6 years old.

Much of my Father's work was carried out on the platforms or rostrums of Spiritualist Churches at Aldershot, Fleet, Alton, Basingstoke, Farnham and Camberley. This restricted area was due to the fact that we lived in a small village called Ash which was fairly central to the towns mentioned but as he couldn't drive then we had to rely on the available public transport which was the good old bus service. You can imagine what sort of service a small village would have, especially on a Sunday. You were lucky if they arrived hourly, if at all, so it was somewhat a labour of love in itself just to get himself to a church. My Father always worked in deep trance, which was not, and still today is not that common an occurance. As you can imagine he was always so well received, mainly because this sort of church work is a little out of the ordinary but also

I believe because the addresses given by his guide were so beautiful. The guide who looked after the clairvoyance part of the service was a venerable Chinese gentleman whose name was *Lau-Hoo*, and as far as I can recall he was always accurate and managed to get the message across to the recipient.

Last but certainly not least, was a gentle guide who gave us philosophy of a higher order. He was resposible for the many wonderful addresses given to the capacity filled churches and at the privately held seminars that he was asked to attend.

As previously mentioned, I was too young to appreciate the knowledge that was brought down to us by *Sunshine* during my earlier years. Thankfully though several of *Sunshines* addresses were tape-recorded for my father to listen to because he was never fully aware of what was being said or happening whilst he was in trance. I was lucky enough to obtain copies of these recordings from my mother and through listening to these addresses, on numerous occassions, I have come to realise much of the golden knowledge which is contained within his works. It is through his words that I have rediscovered and enhanced my belief in the continuance of life from this mortal coil into the world of spirit. I have no strong religious beliefs, in the orthodox sense of the word, but I do have a quiet, unshakeable faith in spirit which has been confirmed to me and my family time and time again. The following passages explain that first and foremost we are of spirit, that there is a spirit world, how it works, where it is and why we are here. For me it has been a case of, 'Those who have eyes to see, will see and those who have ears to hear, will hear,' because finally everything has fallen into place and it all seems to make sense to me. Hopefully these passages that follow will at least give you food for thought, but I am sure that you will receive so much more. I have tried to keep the following four passages in a progressive order for you but I think you will find that all four passages will give you the same fundamental message. That you are first and foremost of spirit and that you are only at the beginning of your true life. If only more of us could accept and learn to realise that we are in fact a spirit with a body and not a body with a spirit. At the end of the addresses given by *Sunshine* there are several more poems written by my father but inspired from spirit and each one of them is like a personal tribute of his feeling for his guides and those in spirit. Following on from that there is an address given by *Mahanka*, his healer, about healing.

But first I would like to open, as *Sunshine* always did, with the following prayer.

SUNSHINES' PRAYER

Spirit of Light, thou who has said that when two or three are gathered in thy name, that thou wouldst be in their midst. We do ask thee to bless us with thy presence at this very moment of time.
We ask thee to bless, O Father God, all these loved ones here gathered, each according to their needs. We ask thee to bless, O Father God, all those loved ones who are sick and that are suffering, that they may be healed and may be comforted.
We ask thee to bless, O Father God, all those loved ones that are in darkness, that it may be made light for them.
We ask thee to bless, O Father God, all those small souls that are entering into this earthplane at this very moment of time, that their pathway through this earthspan may be made right.
We ask thee, O Father God, also to bless all those loved ones that are entering into spirit at this very moment of time. That they may be met by their loved ones, and the silent ones who have guided them through lifes long journey, so they might understand. We ask thee to bless, O Father God, all the leaders of the nations of this earthplane. Bless them with thy wisdom O Father God and let them use it accordingly. We ask Thee to bless, O Father God, all the youth of this earthplane, they who are begining to turn to thee. All these things we do ask in the name of Christ thy Son. AMEN

ADDRESSES BY SUNSHINE

1. THE SPIRIT WORLD
2. THE SEVEN SPHERES
3. LIFE IN SPIRIT
4. THE CYCLE OF LIFE

POEMS ATTRIBUTED TO SPIRIT

1. MEDITATION
2. GOD
3. MAN'S BIRTHRIGHT
4. CHRIST
5. SPIRITUAL AWAKENING

ADDRESS BY MAHANKA

1. HEALING

THE SPIRIT WORLD

I want to give you the materialistic version relating to the world of spirit and also the religious or the spiritual version relating to the world of spirit.
There are many among you who have had experience and understand, and there are those of you who have not the experience and do not understand.
In the first place we must help you to fully understand that there is a spirit world and the only way we can relate this to you is by refering to myself, who is standing here before you, not totally incarnate in the medium's body, but simply impinging at the back of his neck and tapping into it like a telephone wire. In other words, at the base of the skull there is a mass, like a block, which would be like a sub-station or a junction box. This is putting it crudely, putting it in a picture form for you to understand it. In actual fact we break through the nervous system, tapping into the nerves that relay messages to the medium's brain, thereby, incorporating our own movements, our own speech and our own thoughts. The impulses that go to the medium's brain are ours. When we try to teach newcomers about the realms of spirit, we have to inform them of this you see and then we have to tell them that first and foremost, that they are of spirit. Of course, as you know from your good book, at the very beginning when God created the earthplane, the heavens above and indeed the whole universe, He saw it and was pleased. And he decided that he would like to share his love of this earthplane. So he created man, and he created man in his own image. God is spirit, a divine spirit that existed before the

great creation. God, who had put together a master plan, like a gigantic jig-saw puzzle, and did create your heavens and earth. And God created man so that he could share his love for this earthplane, and he created man in his own image, being that of spirit. So first and foremost you are of spirit. Then of course God had to give you a vehicle to transport you to this earthplane from the spirit world, so he gave you a physical body. This is because you are living in a physical plane of thought and you have to have a physical vehicle to maintain this status quo. Why did he have to do this? And why are we here? We are here to perform a service to God and that is, to create a physical world that would be a Heaven on Earth, and have no doubt, that in time this will happen. Before any of this can happen, people who are not in the right frame of mind must be taught and led to be made aware of the eternal life that lays before them. Now these people have to be taught sometimes in picture form. If they are lucky they may have thoughts of their own and they can relate to these thoughts and can sometimes find their own way. But many of us need to have a picture formed to translate the message for us. Remember how Christ, when he was relating his parables or his teachings to his disciples, he purposely painted them descriptively, in picture form, in a parabolic form, so that his disciples could see for themselves. It is like a plasebo. Many people do not have a great depth of thought and have to have a sugar-coated pill and it takes this sugar-coated pill to help them understand and believe but many people do not believe because they cannot see. Christ, in his teachings, went about transferring his own knowledge that he had of spirit, into a form of understanding that could be understood by all walks of life, be they intellectual or illiterate. He taught them the parable of the prodigal son. Now many of you may have understood this parable and some of you have not. Remember the farmer who had two sons, and one, the younger one, wished to take his share of the father's estate that was due to him so that he could go on his own way and search out life for himself. Meanwhile the elder son stayed with his father. Now the younger son went off on his merry way and did err and stray and many times was found wanting. When he had spent all that had been given to him and had released all those possessions that had been given unto him, he decided to make his way back to his father. And his father did welcome his younger son with open arms and he killed the fatted calf in celebration of his son's return. Now the elder son was terribly disappointed in all this that had happened and he said to his father, "Why hast thou done this," and the reply the father gave unto to his eldest son was, "My son was dead and now he is alive." In other words the father was giving his son another chance. Now all of this was related by Christ, to his disciples, in this form, the parabolic form which has a double meaning. He had already spoken to them and said, "Those of you who have eyes to see, will see, and those of you who have ears to hear will hear." After a while his disciples saw through this little ploy of Christ's, this mental picture that was portrayed to them of the prodigal son. That picture had another meaning The farmer was God, the other son was you, each and every one of you. God is the one who has to turn the other cheek every second of every minute of every hour of every day, to some one or other that takes his name in vain or blasphemes in his name. For God does not reject any of his children. He will turn the other cheek and give you another chance and another chance and another chance, ad-infinitum. This was the story that Christ tried to portray in his parable.

You may also remember the story of the woman who was going to be stoned, the crowd called her an adultress and were about to throw stones at her, and Christ came among them saying, "thou who art without sin, let him cast the first stone." You see, even Christ, who we all think of as All Glory, All Divine, he who most of all could have thrown the first stone did not, because Christ, even in his short life had sinned more than once.

Another time the crowds were talking about a man who had riches and who taxed them, and they were in their element at trying to drag him down with name calling. Christ said to them, "Judge ye not, lest ye be judged." This has the same meaning as he who is without sin casting the first stone. Christ, who was man and solely man, nothing divine about him whilst he traversed this earthplane. He was born of God, as you are all born of God, having been given the divine spark of life when you quicken in your mother's womb. It is up to every one of you what you do with this life, this divine spark which has been given to you. Christ was born of humble beginings which in some cases is a blessing but for others it is not a blessing. But you are able to turn humbleness into a blessing and into humility that goes with it. Christ went into the tabernacle at the age of twelve years and confounded the elders of the church. He was not an unruly child, neither was he a good child because he would play pranks and have fun and sport with the other children of the village. There was within him this divine spark which each and every one, as I have said before, is presented with at birth. It was this divine spark that Christ, at this tender age of twelve years old, began to realise was there. He began to realise that he was of spirit, first and foremost of Spirit, not just simple flesh and blood and bone.

Of course, once that realisation was there in his mind, so spirit drew closer to him and he drew closer to spirit and there was a bond and an understanding much beyond his tender years. Once this realisation came to the fore, he was no doubt coaxed and even developed by his loved ones, his mother, his father and no doubt a few of the elders and maybe one or two other seers or prophets. And like those goodly parents of his, who had spoken with God, or had said that they had spoken with God, because of course they were instruments or mediums of God, as Christ would eventually grow up to be. There were at that time, in that part of the world especially, many beliefs but also

The Sunshine Of My Life

at that time there was a full quota of mediums, prophets and seers. Almost every small village that you came across had it's seer, prophet or medium. If a voice came to them clairaudiently (clear hearing of spirit) or if someone spoke through them whilst they were in a trance and others heard, then they would proclaim it to be the voice of God. It was the voice of God, but spoken through, if you like, a medium in the spirit world, a communicator doing God's will but only because he was a soul that had evolved to a higher level of understanding. It may be that he had only just been within the realms of this earthplane, this first plane of thought. When you first enter into spirit you are not as much related to the spirit as you are to the physical. So therefore you may have more thoughts of the physical but at the same time you can speak, work or inspire from spirit. Of course these people, when they heard these voices, thought it was the voice of God. Christ was the foremost medium of his day. Christ was divine only in as much that we have made him divine. God never made Christ more divine than you or I. It was Christ himself that nurtured the presence within him but also tried to rise to higher and higher levels of understanding. As you know the law of attraction, like attracts like, and so he was able to draw to himself those beautiful, tender souls of spirit that had already evolved to higher Spheres or planes of thought. You may remember, when on the mount, before he gave his beattitudes to us, and before he gave the Lord's Prayer. Remember how humble it was because it was his own prayer, his first words were, 'Our Father,' not, 'My Father,' but, 'Our Father.' Christ even then had learned the lesson of humility. He was walking side by side with guides that reached him, inspired him, talked to him, made him understand, were able to give him the powers of levitation, even control over the elements, making him the perfect medium for all things of the spirit. Those that led him from spirit were every bit as divine as Christ was made divine. Remember on the Mount, the Transfiguration.

The Sunshine Of My Life

On either side of him there stood Elijah and Moses, who had walked this earth many hundreds of years before Christ. In their turn, those prophets of old, were also made divine by their followers and their Disciples. Elijah and Moses transfigured, what was the reason for this, if Christ were so divine he would not need these guides. Christ was not divine, he was simply flesh and bone as you all are but was, fortunate in that at the tender age of twelve, he realised that he was of spirit. Some of this understanding comes to many of us, maybe in not so tender an age, and to some of us it comes much later in life. But come it will, even up to your last day upon this earthplane, it will come. There will be an understanding that you are of spirit. Even if it happens just before you are parted from the silver cord and your spirit body is parted from your physical frame, you will have knowledge of spirit. Many of you have loved ones in spirit and have spoken with them mentally and some times even physically. Some of you have not yet reached a time in your life when it is deemed necessary for you to have this knowledge. Some of you have looked at things in a more material sense of the word, trying to understand the spirit from within and by your own and intellectual thoughts. Maybe you are more fortunate than the rest. But there are those of us, although not illiterate, who have not yet reached a level of understanding where we can cope with this knowledge ourselves. We have to have it illustrated for us, and this is illustrated in the religious or pagan way, through all the rituals, dogmas and creeds that are preached. As I have said before, Christ placed a placebo before his disciples and people still need today a placebo, something they can physically see. Something they can physically hear, either religion, whether it is Muslim, Buddhist, Confucianism or your own religion, all these religions must eventually lead to God. Just because a Buddhist does not believe in Christ, it does not mean to say that he does not believe in the spirit world. Just because a Buddhist does not believe in Christ, it does not mean that he does not believe that he is of spirit. Just because a Buddhist does not believe in Christ, it does not mean that he will be rejected by God, the one and only divine source which all men recognise. They call him by another name like Krishna, Mohammed or Confucius. All mankind has an inbuilt belief in a divine source of life which we term God. God in his infinite wisdom made this creative pattern that he had thought out long before the creation which has given to us many diverse paths of life and understandings. Because variety is the spice of life and life would be very dull if we were all cast in the same mould. As I have said before, that as we begin to realise that first and foremost we are of spirit, then it is up to us how we react to this knowledge, how we evolve. Like attracts like and as you evolve so you will draw to yourselves those who have evolved to a higher state. But those who do not wish to understand but who could understand, will draw to themselves rather indifferent beings, beings that are not evolved and who are quite content to keep those physical thoughts that they had whilst on the earthplane. Those who would be in a kind of limbo, a kind of lethargy, leaving it up to others to do the bidding of God and saying to themselves, "Well all will be right in the end." A much better way is for one who has the realisation that they are of spirit is to reach out, to try and spiral into the ether, to be at one with their God, also with those in spirit who are just waiting and willing to help with their unfoldment. This will stand you in good stead once you have departed from this mortal coil, away from this mundane plane of thought, away from material things. This will help you to a fuller understanding and the realisation that you have found, at last eternal life. A life with no ending, a life that will go on to infinity, a life where you will find that all the aches and pains that you have whilst on the earthplane will disappear, arms or legs that were missing are now whole again. Once you have shed these physical thoughts then you begin to evolve. Very gradually, because you cannot expect to spend a span of life upon this earthplane and then go from being a material being and to then an Angel with wings, because this is not so. When you depart from this earthplane you will find that although you have the advantage of being without pain and being whole again, you will still have physical thoughts. As you gradually lose or shed these thoughts, in the passage of time by your Earth standards, then your evolution begins. Your unfolding begins and you travel away through the spheres to the ultimate, to the divine source of life which is God. But this is another subject, the spheres, which will be discussed at another time.

GOD BLESS YOU.

THE SEVEN SPHERES

I will now take you on a little journey through the spheres. For anyone who does not know what the spheres are, they are the seven planes of thought, wrought by God's will and cosmic law. The first plane of thought is that in which you find yourselves at this very moment in time. From the time that you entered into this earthplane, by God's will, so your life has begun. We all know that this earthplane is a very mundane plane of thought, more material and physical than Spiritual. But, we are all born with spirituality because we are all God's children. When we reach the age of understanding it is up to us how we live our lives. As you know some people have very humble beginings and this helps them with the lesson of humility. Humility is the greatest virtue that there is, because all the other virtues such as Faith, Hope, Charity and Compassion are nothing unless practiced with humility. Therefore if we can understand that we are of the spirit, we can spiral from time to time, reaching out into the ether for spiritual guidance. We might pattern our lives like a flower which is unfolding and then we know we have done well. For it is all according as to how you pattern your life, as to the results which will follow in this later life which we call the spirit world. You all know that you have an alotted time, not a minute sooner or later which you will spend on this earthplane. So it is how you pattern this life that you lead which is the deciding factor when entering into the second phase of thought, which is the Spirit World. You might say to yourself, "What is the spirit world?" "Where is the spirit world?" The answer is that the Earth has an Equator, an invisible line running around the middle, so it is with your physical world and the spirit world. The spirit world is about you, around you, wherever you are. Where there are spirit loved ones, they are standing about you. Every personality, everyone on this earthplane, when they pass into spirit, has an etheric counterpart which is called the spirit body. Even your chairs and cupboards have their own etheric counterparts. You might say, "What is it like living in the spirit world." We try to analyse ways and means of telling you . The nearest to which we can compare is like that of your dreamstate. You have all probably had vivid dreams from time to time and you are quite happy in these dreams.

You see people and personalities that are animated, which have colour, which have depth, which you see in three dimensions and you are quite happy with all of this. Even a blind person has dreams and can see pictures of people, can see people moving about, can see flowers and trees. And that is what is meant by the etheric counterpart, that is the best way I can explain this condition for you. The spirit world is like a dreamstate which everyone has to get used to. As you know, when you pass from this earthly coil you have great ties with earthly and physical contacts, so we do not make the departure so abrupt for you.

If you pass into spirit whilst in a hospital, so in the spirit world there is an etheric counterpart, a hospital, doctors and nurses who take care of you are there also. Those who have taken care of you through your earthly life, including your guides, stay with you until you understand that you are, solely of spirit and until that time you will not meet with your loved ones. This is because the comprehension that you have is indistinguishable between the two worlds and until you have accepted that you are of spirit then you will not be allowed to see your loved ones. You may think that this is all very harsh but in no time at all, when you can accept, then you are allowed to see your loved ones who are in spirit and you are reunited. But you must

The Sunshine Of My Life

understand it all depends on how you have patterned your life as to how readily you accept this condition. Some take longer than others, some take a really long time compared to your standards of earth time.

The drawing of the earthly feelings of life, physical attractions, are all far greater to them than is the spiritual call. These loved ones have to be helped to understand, to be made aware that they have passed into spirit and have left behind their physical body. Sometimes it is very difficult to help them understand and this is when we have to rely upon your loved ones on the earthplane. Those of you who hold rescue circles, because you can help far better than we can in this sort of instance to help them realise that they have passed into spirit.

In due course each and every one of you has to return to God, from whence you came. No matter how long it takes, no matter how adverse you are in your way of thinking, no matter how much you are attached to this earthplane, each one of you has to unfold to the full.

And so we travel through to the third sphere of thought. I want to emphasise to you that it is not like getting into an elevator and going from the first to the seventh floor.

All of these ethereal planes of thought are intertwined so that you would not realise that you were travelling from one plane to another. In other words it would be like when you, on the earthplane, are growing up. With no distinctive going out of one door into another, going from one sphere into another, it is all a very gradual process.

The following is just a short resume of this condition in spirit. If I were to tell you of the various spheres of thought that I have passed through then I would never finish describing all that happens. All the wonderful knowledge and marvelous things that lay in store for you. You do not pass into the third sphere of thought until the acceptance that you are spirit and the will to unfold are with you. Within this third sphere you may have great teachers who will come to you from time to time. There may be some latent desire that you have had to complete some work, be it a writing, music, or even to build a house. These things that you wished to complete in your earthly life may now be accomplished here in the third sphere. The teachers that come to you, come from the sixth sphere of thought, down through the ether, sacrificing much as they draw nearer to your earthplane, but unerringly doing so. These spirit people are ones who are souls of tenderness in hope of humility. They are willing to come down through the ether to this third plane of thought to unfold to you the wonders that lay in store for you. From the third sphere, once the acceptance and the knowledge that you are going to unfold to the utmost of your aspirations is with you, then you travel into the fourth sphere of thought. Now on this plane of thought comes a big decision and the height of spirituality you have achieved up to this time plays a big part. You may either come back to this earthplane as a helper, a control, a communicant or you may travel further onwards and ever upwards to reach the ultimate. This fourth plane of thought is where most of the guides and controls come from. You have a free will, even in spirit. God has not suddenly decided that it will be taken away from you. The free will that was given to you at birth carries on right through your earth lifespan and your Spiritual lifespan.

Even though God would love you to do his will, he wants you to do it of your own free will. So you see you can become a working guide, giving help to those loved ones that are travelling from the earthplane to the world of spirit. Help them to understand in the same way as you have been helped. This does not stop you from progressing because if you decide that you would like to work through an instrument on the earthplane, from the fourth plane of thought, you will sacrifice much by becoming closer to the Earth, but you will not be sacrificing anything of your progression . Once a medium passes into the

The Sunshine Of My Life

world of spirit then your job will be done. Unless of course you decide to take on further work, you would then automatically earn the right to be transferred through the spheres to the fifth plane of thought. Now this fifth plane of thought is where I, *Sunshine*, come from, right on the edge, on the very beginning of this plane of thought.

This is where most of the teachers come from, who travel to your earthplane from time to time, to pass on to you the knowledge that they hold. To give you more understanding. To help you to pattern your lives like a spiritual flower that will unfold. And so greater knowledge is given to them as they reach higher into the fifth sphere of thought.

Much knowledge is sent down through the ether and the higher you spiral the more knowledge, the more philosophy there is to be unfolded, not only to the loved ones on the earthplane but also to those in the lower realms of spirit.

There are also great halls of learning and beautiful souls that teach us. Even those prophets of old come to us and unfold to us the mysteries of life, the meaning of God, the meaning of love, the meaning of why he gave his only begotten son that we might live.

These souls come from the sixth sphere and it is at this point, when one is established within this sphere, that there is no return. Only communication with those on the highest level of spirituality, receiving entire absolution of sin and of anything physical that remains.

We do not know what happens on the seventh sphere because we have not reached that condition yet. We understand from these prophets of old, we enter the Kingdom of God.

We come as a seed of divinity and we have born fruit and we have become as a seed once again. We have come to the God head, we have come to all that is beautiful, all that is love, all that is powerful, the nucleus of divinity. We have performed an eternal circle of life. We have come through the spheres of

The Sunshine Of My Life

thought. We have come from God and returned to God. The continuance of life goes on. Some of these seeds are set aside and may return again, but that is another story.

GOD BLESS YOU.

LIFE IN SPIRIT

On this occasion we are to talk about life in spirit. First and foremost I want to explain to you exactly what we mean by the spirit world. No doubt some of you have seen the spirit world depicted in paintings, symbolic drawings or other such idiums that one would like to exercise. In many of these paintings you will see the spirit world split up into seven spheres or seven planes of thought. Now when one in the physical body, as you are, looks at these paintings and wonders, I believe first and foremost you are intrigued. Then you have nagging doubts and think to yourself, how do I get from there to up there. By the time you reach the top of the painting or the seventh sphere it all looks too good for you. Well I can tell you here and now, nothing is too good for you or for anybody else. Many of you have wondered about what happens to you. Those of you who believe in survival, who believe in the spirit world, still wonder, or are afraid. Even though you have the knowledge of this parting phase, this disinheriting of your physical body to spiral into the ether of the spirit world. I want to make it easy for you and understandable to you, so I will try to explain it to you in this way. The spirit world has no geographical position. It is here and now and all around and about you. If you could see with your psychic eye you would find that your loved ones, who are in spirit, have come to stand beside you. There are also guides and controls all about you who are just as interested in you and what you believe in as what they believe. Now in the first instance you are of God because you are born in his image and created in his image. So first and foremost you are of spirit but you are spirit that is incarnate in a physical body. You are all aware of this I am sure but first of all the spirit has to enter into the body and this is done by the process of birth. The seed is formed and then the embryo begins to grow and it becomes a foetus. Then the child quickens within the mother's womb and so the spirit enters. Then the child comes from the mother's womb and is born. Now being born is a wonderous time for everyone concerned. It brings an awareness of spirit because when one looks upon the face of newborn child, they would be lying if they said they felt nothing. It is a spiritual moment because you are looking on the face of a newborn spirit. This can be likened to arriving in the first plane of thought in the spirit world. You go there after passing from your physical body at the moment of your earth death. You enter the spirit world and just like as a child, there is wonderment at what you find. And as you grow up as a child, you would be inquisitive, you ask questions. It would be the same as you would be doing in the spirit world, you would be looking around, asking questions and finding out things. This would take you from one plane of thought to another. And as you grow up on the earthplane, so you would grow up in spirit and there would be more understanding and knowledge. And when you reach the third phase or the third plane of thought in your earth life, so you would reach the third plane of thought or third sphere in your spirit life. It is all a matter of growing up. It is just a simple matter of awareness and of spirituality. Then when you reach manhood you have sorted out your life as to what you want to do. The same applies in spirit because you have accumulated knowledge and you will be set on a path of regression or digression. This would follow you through your spirit life, as it would follow you through your physical life.

So you can see there are no stepping stones, just a gradual continuation of life and that is what it is like in the spirit world. You need not pass into spirit with a feeling of fear, when you pass into spirit you find that you will maintain the same conditions that pertained when you left. When you pass to spirit through an illness, you will find that when you enter into spirit that you will still be ill and you will have spirit doctors and spirit nurses who would bring you through your illness just like the doctors and nurses would on the earthplane. There would be a period of convalescence. There is nothing that God would place upon you such as fear. It is as natural as the life that you are leading now, at this very moment of being incarnate. If you have feelings of guilt before passing into spirit, so you will still have the same feeling of guilt as you enter spirit. If you have feelings of love when you pass, so you will still have feelings of love. If you are in the depths of despair, then so shall you be down in the depths of despair when in spirit. But there are those who have walked with you on your life's journey upon this earthplane who have watched over you and at different times have inspired you to do this or not to do that, who will be waiting for you. They will be the first ones who will meet you in spirit, once you have become aware that you are in spirit. How can I say what Spirit is. All I can say is, as you have come from God so shall you return to God. I cannot put a name to God other than to say that God is the divine power who rules the entire Universe, with law and order. There is a law and order in your heavens, there is a law and order on your plane and there is a law and order in spirit. In other words cosmic law continuously flows throughout the entire cosmos and that includes the spirit world. Although you cannot see spirit, unless your psychic eye is open, it is still part of the cosmos but in a different dimension of life. You are living now in one dimension and the spirit world is another dimension. It is the same as when you grow up from babyhood to youth to manhood to maturity to middle age and to old age, they are all different dimensions. They do not come upon you suddenly, they are a gradual process, as is the the process of the cycle of life. From whence you came so shall you return. This is what it is like in the spirit world, as for the environment, I do not understand what you mean by environment in the spirit world. The environment is a physical word and not a spiritual one. If you mean where does one live or in what habitat, well as you already know 'in my Father's house there are many mansions.' There will be many of you who will understand this and there are many who will not understand it. As in your own physical existence upon this earthplane you have many personalities and each one of you are a different personality. You all have times in a world of your own and then you look outside and there are many people outside who live in a world of their own. No two people are alike. Each birth that happens on your earthplane is a virgin birth. It is a virgin birth because it has never happened before and it will never happen again, that is one of the gifts of God. But also the gift of God is the spark of divinity that he has given to each and every one of us, that spark of divinity is of himself. He has given part of himself to you. You are part of God and it depends on all of you as to what you do with this spark of life, light, or divinity that has been given to you. It depends on you as to whether you would like to nurture or destroy it. This can be done, sometimes even by people other than yourself who will try to destroy your spirit. While you have a free will, you have the free will to do with yourself as you would wish. If you are one who is aware of spirit you understand what is going to happen to you eventually. You are going to leave this physical world of thought and enter into a more beautiful situation which is the spirit world. Here you will be able to shed off all these physical attributes and material thoughts, which takes time to do. That is why I say to you that when you come into spirit it is not a fearsome time but just a continuance of life. How do we travel in spirit? Well you have all been aware at some time or other, or have had experience of this. In your dimension you may have had examples of this yourself. How many of you have sat and meditated, or mused whilst laying in bed, and in your minds eye you have seen a place that you have visited. It looks in your minds eye to be as solid as when you were there. This you will find can only be done for a split second of time because you are living in a physical plane of thought and it is impossible to retain this picture. But once you leave your body and are in spirit then this is your method of travel. Projection, thought projection. Thought, that is the most powerful thing in the entire cosmos. It took thought, by the divine power, to plan out this beautiful earthplane and all that it contains. Also your heavens in the sky, your own marvelous planetary system, your galaxy and all the outer galaxies. So you must never, never belittle the power of thought. Just try to imagine what thought went into the creation, even before the creation took place. It is so vast a thing to try and comprehend, but you can always take a blade of grass and look at it's structure, discovering that it also is created by God. When you look at a blade of grass you are also looking at the entire cosmos.

So I would say to you that travelling in the spirit world is a thing that is learned much more easily than you would understand. Because once you have left your physical body and are able to spiral into the ether you become aware that you have passed over and have got used to this idea of travel by thought projection, so you think and you will be there. The same conditions apply to food. I know food is a physical thing and I expect you think, "Why do we have to have food." Well as long as it is necessary for you to have food then this will be taken in thought form, but to the one who has just been initiated into spirit this would seem real. Gradually you will have those in spirit who will come and advise you and expound to you and explain to you different things. So eventually you will become aware, and you will gradually shed these physical thoughts that cling to you because of your time upon the earthplane. Gradually these feelings will leave you and the new dimension that you find yourself in will become as natural to you as the earthplane. Nothing at all to be afraid of, just a simple continuance of life. You might think it's all very well for him to say that, but with all the knowledge that you possess and garner unto yourself, there is still a fear of the unknown. That is why I have been asked to come and speak with you on this subject, to help alay your fears. Also I say to you, there is a better time coming for all of you and this good time is a time to prepare yourself for. To become aware that you are part of God and for you to try and do his will with the free will that he has given you. Of course God wants you to do his will, of course God would like us to be as spiritual as he is. For the simple reason that you are part of God and he does not want the part of him he has given to you to be thrown away and wasted. Because when you enter into spirit, if you have become a materialist and you love matter rather than spirit then you would dwell upon physical thoughts all of the time. This is not going to help you one little bit, because you will find that you will have more physical attributes to disavow yourself of before you can achieve any progression or evolution. There are those on your earthplane who reach a very low depth and when passing into spirit would not believe for one moment that they had died. They would not allow those in spirit, who have tried to walk with them on the earthplane, to come anywhere near them, they would just poo-poo the idea and send their silent friend packing. That is even if they could be reached in the first place by by these silent ones. They would just keep reaching out for the physical and become more or less what you call earthbound as they could not do without physical or material things. So therefore I tell you, my children, if you are aware of the spirit that is within you then nurture it well because it will stand you in good stead. What kind of place do we live in, what sort of habitat? Well again, it depends on the awareness of spirit within you. If you are a person who has led a hum-drum sort of life, who would never reach the heights of merriment, or if you have never had a day that has been different one from another, then you will find that you will need to live in a house which will be there for you on your arrival. This will be needed all the time that you cling to the physical and your earthly life. But everyone evolves in spirit, so all these physical things are eventually discarded and gradually we become spiritualy purer and purer. That is when you will find that you are travelling through different spheres of life in spirit, through different planes of thought, because thought is the essence of spirit throughout the seven spheres. And as the thought improves so the spirit improves and you reach out and eventually your journey will finish in the place from whence it began, from God and back to God.

GOD BLESS YOU.

THE CYCLE OF LIFE

The reading tonight portrays the spirit world as something of a dream-like world. The instrument through whom these words were spoken was an instrument of high standing who oozed love and received love in just as great a quantity. The guide who spoke through this sister, whose pseudonym was *Zodiac*, was a speaker in the temple, at the time of Christ. Now the portrayal of the spirit world given, some of you might be able to accept but for some of you who are new to this movement it becomes intangeable. Therefore I am going to give a short resume on the spirit world in comparison with your own world, this physical plane of thought. It was described in the reading that the beings in spirit were not of a molecular structure, of course they are not because they are simply of spirit. So first and foremost I must try to explain to you what is meant by spirit. If you have read your good book, I am sure that most of you at one time or another have done so, then you will have begun at the beginning, with Genesis. It goes on to say how God created the firmament, the earth, the seas, the fishes and the fowl, and then God created man. God created man in his own image. Now God being of spirit, therefore man was made in God's own image which is spirit. So first and foremost you are of Spirit. God in his infinite wisdom created this Earthplane. You must imagine that it was not done willy-nilly, but that a lot of forethought, positive and creative had gone into it so that all should fit together like a gigantic puzzle, complementing the other pieces that each adjoined. God so loved this earthplane, this garden of eden that he had created, he decided that he would like to share this love and so he created man and womb-man (woman). There is a physical garment that you all wear and that is your body, but within that physical body there is an etheric body which is called the spirit and that is the spirit that God created. That is the man which God created in his own image. The physical body simply allows you to dwell on this earthplane, soaking up and taking in all the knowledge and understanding that is within ones capacity. We all have a span of life that we must live and within that span of life you will be able to do what you want to. The spirit body has to take in all that it can whilst it is on the earthplane, so that it will suffice when you return to the spirit from whence you came. Because there is a cycle of life which is a law, a natural law, everything in this physical plane of thought, and even in the world of spirit, works in a cycle. You come from God, from spirit, down through the ether into the earthplane to inhabit a child's body. Then to go through this physical span of life, stage by stage, finishing in the spirit world and going through that without the physical body, back from where you came. Some of you might think that this all sounds very high and fallacious, but it is so. I want to now take you on a journey through your own life span, in comparison to the span of life you must expect after you have finished your understandings on this mortal coil. You are born on this earthplane as a spiritual being. All of you have, I know at one time or another, gazed down upon the face of a small newborn baby and looked into it and have seen nothing but love and spirituality. Even unto seeing the knowledge therein and having, sometimes, to avert your gaze from that spiritual being because it is so bright and so spiritual. This is because it has not been long removed from the God Head.

You all know that when within the mother's womb the child quickens. The breath of life enters into the child, that is the time that the divine spark of life, the spirit, enters into the foetus and becomes a child, becomes a living being, even though it has not yet been born. Then you are born and your life begins. The child begins to look about and tries to visualise and use their eyes correctly to determine what it is that they see. The same applies to the first stage of your life in spirit. You enter into the world of spirit, as but a child, because you have no knowledge of the spirit world and you look about and you try to focus your eyes. Some things may seem frightening to you, some things will seem pleasant to you and then your eyes will become accustomed to their new surroundings. Then you look for someone that you will feel an affinity to, which would be your mother here on the earthplane. If it be that your mother has passed into the spirit world before you then it is her you will look for again, but it could be anyone that you love. Now this is all on the first plane of thought because the two worlds intermingle at that stage, the first plane of thought in spirit and here on the earthplane. Then we acquire a little knowledge in our own mind as a child and as a child in spirit. I am not saying that you are going to become as a little child but your knowledge will be the same as a little child when you enter in to spirit because it will all be so new. Then you grow up in stages and as you grow up so you receive more and more knowledge. Now we all have tuition, or an inner tutor, or intuition that tells us the difference between right and wrong. Some people call it the conscience, some people call it a deep understanding, but all it is is a level you have reached at that moment of time. It is a level of awareness, a level of understanding, the feeling of spirit instilled within you.

The same will apply in the spirit world because you gain knowledge along with your further understanding. As you tread this mortal coil, your life unfolds before you, there are seven stages of man so there are seven planes of thought in the spirit world, each intermingling with one another. As you have an affinity with a loved one, so there is an affinity with you from the world of spirit. Your level of awareness unfolds to a greater ego, an ego which is the soul or mind of the spirit. How do we determine the answers that are forthcoming, as we dwell upon various things whilst meditating, that is if we even leave enough time for ourselves to meditate. This world progresses so materialism becomes that much greater and the spiritual side of us seems to take a secondary place. Therefore, if we are in a situation where we do not come into contact with those things of the spirit, then we are inclined to drift, ebb and flow over life's surface understanding nothing of the spirit. Not knowing which way, or even whether, to go on. But you can rest assured that at long as you have the spirit within you, that there is going to come a time, in each of your lives, when you will be made aware of spirit. Be it at a young and tender age in your childhood or in the evening of your life, because God is not a vengeful God. He will not hurl you headlong into the world of spirit without a foretaste or foreknowledge of that spirit. You have all heard that when people are on their beds of sickness, not only the old but also the young, they have visions. They see clearly with their inner eye, the psychic eye, pictures of loved ones who have passed. Or you may even have knowledge passed onto you in a split second, an instant of time. There is no recapturing that picture no matter how hard you try, that is how the spirit world works. There are two seperate entities, the physical and the spiritual, for there to become a Heaven on Earth, a Garden of Eden, a Brotherhood of Man, then these two worlds must blend together, right together. So spirit makes certain sure that before you reach that stage of life, or before your span of life is end, then we make sure that you have had instruction or a picture form of knowledge of the world of spirit. No doubt many of you have seen elderly people on their beds of sickness, just before their spirit has left its physical shell, they see people that they have known during their earthly life, who have passed on before them. So you see even the elderly, even if they have gone right the way through their life without an introduction to spirit, then they will get it at the end of their physical life so that they will not feel lost when they do enter the spirit world. This unfoldment, this life of understanding that lays before all of you, depends solely on the way your spiritual unfoldment evolves. It is no good reading a piece of knowledge or having a piece of knowledge unfolded to you unless you analyse it. It is no good letting it go in one ear and out of the other. It is up to you to do something about it because it is a two way effort and the two worlds have to be blended to be perfect. As you go through this physical span of life you will reach this level of awareness and each of you as you traverse this lifespan will have thoughts, deep thoughts, positive thoughts, creative thoughts, some disruptive thoughts, which are all generated into the ether because thoughts are energy, waves of energy, and they remain in the ether. If there are enough creative thoughts, which are energy, then this energy can become mass, it means something. It is like a man who first made a brick to build a house, the creative thought had to be there before it could be formed. And you will have these thoughts.

It all depends entirely on what level of understanding you reach during this physical life as to what you inherit the earth with when you leave. There are those that come after you that will have to go through the same procedures as you have. If you leave your loving thoughts in the ether then they are there for those who follow after to pick up on. To perform this miracle of a brotherhood of man, a Garden of Eden, to return this earthplane that God loves so, as it was in the begining, then these thoughts must turn to love. So now you can see how important each one of you is. None of you are born without that spark of energy, no matter how high or low your birth. Each one of you has been given this divine spark, this little part of God. You are made of his own image, each of you is a little part of God. So it is up to each and every one of you how you nurture, how you tend, how you lovingly care for this spark. This little part of God, because eventually that little part of God has to return from whence it came, it must return to the source of all love and divinity, it must return to the God Head. If you have sinned, erred and strayed from the narrow path and have been found wanting you know you have done wrong. Your Father God, no matter how much you sin, blaspheme and take his name in vain, he will turn the other cheek time and time and time again. Even as Christ preached that we should turn the other cheek, so your Father God will do that until you return home to him. But do not look to him for salvation, do not look to God for forgiveness, do not ask God Oh please forgive me. Instead use that little part of God that is within each and every one of you to forgive yourself. If you find that it is against your conscience to do that then the only other thing that one can do, if you are reaching out of the darkness trying to see the light, is to begin to forget oneself and to love another. Try to perform each day, during a certain minute of the day, a token of brotherly love. The most difficult of these tokens that one can perform is to forgive those that have sinned against you, so that in turn you might be forgiven. That is the way that one can work towards this forgiveness and once you have forgiven yourself then you will find that God has also. There are seven stages of man as I have already explained to you, from babyhood to childhood, youth, manhood, middle age, the age of total awareness or maturity and then of course the evening of life, old age. That is the seven stages of man. Now in spirit there are seven planes of thought. You know that as you go through your earth life that the stages you pass through are not like simple stepping stones that you can determine one from the other, it is a simple transition through our life, it applies the same in the spirit world. You go through the stages of looking around and gaining knowledge and understanding and then reach the age of maturity or total awareness and then by the evening of your life you could possibly be on the sixth plane of thought . Where there is a point of no return, as there is a point of no return when you reach old age. It is a miracle of being, it is a cycle of life, even as your Sun and Solar system traverse around your Galaxy and your planets traverse around your Sun, it is a cycle. For everything, from the spirit world as well as on the earthplane, there is a natural law. This law that has to be obeyed is the cycle of life and each of you has that in front of them. Part of it has already passed. Look forward to the future. Say to yourself, 'I have a new understanding and this I must do something about because it is up to Me.'

GOD BLESS YOU.

MEDITATION

In the stillness of a quiet hour
We ask thee for sufficient power
To spiral from this Earthly Plane
That we might in knowledge gain
From those who are in higher thought
So we might gain from what is taught
To understand the ways of Love
Sent down to us from up above
To feel the presence of those so dear
And the loved ones that draw near
To feel the touch of a childlike hand
To be encircled by a Band
A Band made up from every Nation
That brings to us the radiation
Of the Love their nearness brings
That helps us dwell on Heavenly things
Like a pool of Spirituality
And learning the lesson of Humility
Humility that gives the Soul elation
Needed in this hour of meditation.

GOD...

O God the Father of all men
Who wrought the elements so to blend
Those beautiful Heavens in the sky
And a world so pleasing to the eye

The Sunshine Of My Life

A miracle, no man could comprehend
For Thou art the beginning and the end
O God who gave the Sabbath day
That we might stop upon the way
Of life's long journey, to gaze with awe
On wonderous things made by Thy Law
The Law that governs this plane of thought
The Law that Jesus through Thee taught
That Father God is the Holy Power
Who grants us sweet life hour by hour
So we might know when we hear Thy call
That Thou art Father God of All.

MAN'S BIRTHRIGHT

God instilled in all mankind
Himself, so that all should find
Their true salvation which is God's Will
That they may in Him, themselves instill
For He is the beginning and the end
And all these thoughts of His do blend
Creator of the world and man
He pieced together the Master Plan
A plan much older than Creation
A plan to give us our Salvation
And give to us the jubilation
Of peace on Earth for every Nation
A peace that no man shall disrupt
Nor yet one man another corrupt
All warlike things put on a Pyre
Lit to welcome the new Messiah.

CHRIST

A child was born, the Christ was here
The Son of God, who nought should fear
For He had come to show the light
And teach how to fight the fight
He taught the ways and laws of God
And promised life of eternal beauty
To those who love their fellow men
And who to God did do their duty
Although his stay with us was short
God's words, through Christ, to us were taught
Expounded completely and to the full
He gave the world His golden rule
A rule to give us Heavenly wealth
By loving your brethren as yourself
Christ healed the sick and raised the dead
Yet on the cross for us He bled
His works and life on Earth were done
Father God did welcome His only Son.

SPIRITUAL AWAKENING

Like the Sun of a Summers morning
There is a birth of a new Soul dawning
A Soul that to us did give His all
Yea even to the very call
That God His Father did him give
So we who sinned Him still might live
Live so we might understand
That there is for us a better land
A land much older than creation
Where truly we might find salvation

The Sunshine Of My Life

But surely, surely we must fight
Fight the good fight with all our might
So the Spirit that is within us all
May be worthy when we hear the call
We must spread the word of Brotherly Love
And pray for guidance from above
That we might lead this world so old
Into a mantle of Spiritual Gold
Sheltered from evil by God's own awning
Like the Golden Sun of a summers morning
A world so true and pure within
Truly ready, for He that cometh in.

MAHANKA

As mentioned in the opening chapters, there was a rather remarkable Blackfoot Indian, who was accepted by our family as a Grandfather and who was responsible for many wonderful healings. Be it for the family, for friends or for total strangers who had been introduced by previously helped patients. *Mahanka* was the name by which we knew him although it was not his birth-name. We asked on numerous occasions for him to tell us his birth name, but he would always retort that if he did tell us, that we wouldn't remember it anyway and besides he was known as *Mahanka* and preferred it to remain so. In his own Blackfoot language the word *Mahanka* translates 'The Healer.' He was in fact medicine-man to his people when on the earthplane some 300 years ago. There was one occasion when he did agree to divulge his birth name, and guess what? For the life of me I cannot remember what it was and neither can my mother or sisters. But then I guess I shouldn't be so surprised should I.
Mahanka was also my father's doorkeeper (head of his band) and it was he who led the procedures during home and contact circles. He would generally open with a short talk relating to a subject which he had attended at a seminar in the spirit world. This was done to help put newcomers at their ease before their loved ones arrived, thus creating a more conducive atmosphere for everyone. Unfortunately, during these less formal occasions, the tape recorder was rarely used. It was considered that too many personal messages would be forthcoming and it wasn't the right thing to do to record them. Not only that, but on the

occasions we did try to tape the procedings, nothing ever came out clearly on the tapes, even though it always worked properly at other times.

It is difficult, therefore, to remember much of what was talked about but these short talks did cover a variety of subjects including space travel, which had been debated by scientists in the spirit world and relayed to us, as best as possible by *Mahanka*. His talks included such beliefs as, that no physical space ships have, as of yet, visited our planet. That objects seen in the night sky are more likely to be 'thought projections' or 'thought transferences' from a more spiritually advanced life-form on other planets. As discussed in *Sunshine's* talk on Life in Spirit, travel in spirit is achieved by simply thinking about where you want to be. Therefore, if these beings are are highly advanced they could feasibly project their spirit or even a vehicle image to visit this earthplane in. Also that man will one day achieve space travel at approximately the speed of light, thus being able to visit places where no man has been before - beam me up Scotty! Apparently this might be achieved by using a 'Proton- Drive' vehicle. First of all man will need to harness these 'Protons.' Unfortunately there is, as of yet, no known substance available to man which can hold these 'Protons.' The only substance known to spirit is the mother's womb which provides near perfect protection for the new spirit entering into the new baby at the quickening stage of its life here on this earthplane.

He also discussed the theory that mother nature holds in her vast storehouse, a cure for all known disease. This includes cancer which has its cure, if you like, contained within a common herb in the hedgerow. He could not, and would not, divulge the source because as he explained it is up to man to discover these things for himself. But that someone, somewhere, is working on this theory and that when the time is right that person will be given a nudge, if necessary, in the right direction to discover the cure. As explained, *Mahanka's* talks were generally confined to home and contact circles, helping to put newcomers at their ease. There was one occasion when he agreed to give a talk on the subject of healing, followed by a questions and answers session afterwards. This was taped for my father to listen to at his leisure once he had returned home. Fortunately I have a copy of the tape which has been transcribed into the following text for anyone to learn from, who wishes to do so. In keeping with the previous chapters of *Sunshine's* work, the words written here are the words spoken by *Mahanka*. I hope they give you as much encouragement as they have given to me.

"It seems as though we have been asked to talk to you tonight about the subject, which I am sure most of you are interested in, and that is healing. I wonder what enters your mind when the word 'healing' is pronounced. There are many forms of healing and there are many ways in which they are carried out.
Some of these healings are many thousands of years old but nevertheless they are healings.
There is the ancient art of acupuncture which is healing and remember, that before acupuncture could have been performed, there would have to have been some-one or some creative thought, that told the person who first used needles for acupuncture the exact points where the needles were to be inserted. Now we all know what is Ying and Yang, I expect many of you do, but for those who are unsure Ying and Yang are ease and dis-ease, or disease. Before this acupuncture was performed it was done by mans own fingers, so that takes the actual spiritual healing that you all know back at least to that era. Healing by the fingers or the hands, now a lost art. Many people of that time were initiated into this art of healing by the hands. It became lost in ideology, rites, rituals or whatever you care to call it, as was most of the healing techniques that were

used on this plane. You will find not only with acupuncture, but also Prahmar, where the term Chakra is used, and also will find it with the Spiritual healers; that they all have an unusual awareness and will all go to those seven major spots of the physical body. They will go upon these more or less by instinct if they are inspirational healers. It might be a different matter if one is overshadowed or controlled, but you will find that these points appertain to various glands within the human body and the glands are essential for physical life. Not only for procreative life, such as the prostate and the ovaries, but also for life-giving blood which is work the glands of the body perform. Of course in most cases the glands take substances from the blood and produce Enzymes which have a particular job to do within the physical body.

Spirit healing, you will find, is mainly concerned with these glands and these are in the same area where the acupuncturist or the person that uses Prahmar, will go to in order to carry out their healing work. That is to the Pancreas, to the Thyroid glands, the Pituitary, the Adrenal glands, the Lymphatic glands, the Ovaries and the Prostate gland. These are the KEY centres of the physical body. It doesn't matter how you heal, as long as the person who is going to be healed receives the benefit. You will find that it is possible to heal even through autosuggestion, that is verbal healing. Even through hypnotism which is a way in which autosuggestion is carried out. It does not matter how a person is healed as long as they do receive some benefit from it. What I have to tell you now is essential because I feel that *all* people are potential healers. We all have this energy inherent within us, each and every one of us. I know that you have had other speakers, speaking to you through this medium, who have said this before - that when a case of doubt arises in the mind then who are we to look to, if we cannot find the answer within ourselves. And they have also told you that first and foremost, that you are of spirit. There is the physical body, there is the spiritual body and there is the mind. The mind that is needed to carry this span of life, that the physical body has to traverse. And for one who has doubts in their mind then there is no healing forthcoming, because if one has doubt then that is not harmony. Where there is disharmony you will find that it is not condusive to good healing or good anything else. Scepticism has to be removed, thoughts of the day have to be removed, indeed every physical condition that you suffer during the course of the day has to be removed. For one has to make the channel that the healing is going to flow through as pure as one can. So, therefore, we find that relaxation is the art or the basis of all good healing. Relaxation - some find relaxation in strenuous effort, some find relaxation by sitting quietly, but in each case one has to learn to be able to disperse the mundane thoughts that have gathered in our minds during the course of the day, otherwise healing will not flow. This is because there is a breach within the body, there is disharmony. One way that one can relax is to give oneself to spirit. Make sure that when you attempt this, if you are already giving healing, that you ask for the help of spirit. This is because the energy that is within you or around you, the auric body, this electro-magnetic healing or ray that is surrounding you, or as some would call it the Bio-Plasmic body, each and every one of you has, some greater than others and that is because you are more aware of spirit.

The human body itself generates this electric current of light and if you could see clairvoyantly, you would be able to see it around a persons head, in fact around the whole of the person. This is the *Physical* healing that is inherent within each and every one of you. But, when we need to boost the rays that we are generating, or the power that we are generating, this has to be boosted from outside the physical body and the closer that you can come to spirit, the higher graduation of power or healing that will be fulfilled. One can just merge ones hands with another persons body, simply by impinging upon the aura of that person, not even touching them, maybe an inch or so away. And where there is a lack of energy, so possibly there is also a dis-ease around the whole body. With your own thoughts you send and emit this healing to that loved-one to make them feel better. But if there is not enough power within your own physical body then you will find that by becoming closer to spirit, spirit is always there, and will bolster that healing power by ten fold or even by one hundred fold, so that there can be formed even a regeneration of tissue that has degenerated, a regeneration of blood-cells within the body, even of flesh, and of the nucleus of substances that are within the glands of the body. This is all done in co-operation with the spirit world. So, therefore, you will find that the art of relaxation will enhance the spiritual gift of healing.

The way in which one performs this art of relaxation would be simply to sit on a chair as this medium is doing tonight. If there are no arms on the chair, just lay your hands one upon the other upturned in your lap, having your feet close together and then breath in. Breath in through the inner nostrils, not to just sniff the air but to breath it in through the inner nostrils and to breath in deeply and plentifully. In other words not the shallow breathing that you are doing during the course of the day but to fill your lungs with God's given air, thereby taking in the oxygen that the body requires.

The body requires oxygen not only to oxygenate the blood but also the cells of the body, especially of the head. That then gives you a clear channel, a channel that is in harmony. If you are not receiving oxygen, if it is not reaching your blood, if it is not reaching your brain cells, the air is not incorporated in your lungs, so that you might give your body to spirit, you will find that your body is in disharmony. And as we have said before if there is disharmony or you are unable to relax, so the barrier is set up and healing will not flow. Therefore, the first requisite of healiing is to be at onement with yourself, first and foremost at onement between the mind and the physical body. And then to send your mental thoughts out whilst you are in this state of at onement that you have created for yourself.

If you find it difficult or are unable to relax, begin at the feet and the toes and think of them and wiggle them about, then relax the toes. Then you can think of the instep, the ball of your foot, the arches, the heel, making sure they are all relaxed. Then go to the ankle, to the back part of your legs, to your knees, to the thighs and to go all the way up your body, even to your head. Once you have reached your head, harmony should just about be achieved. You will find that during the time taken, that with practice, this is an essential part of development, you will find that you will achieve at onement. You will sit there in contemplation or meditation, call it what you will, and you can meditate on the subject which is nearest and dearest to you, which might be healing. Or you can always leave yourself open for inspiration which comes from spirit, down through the ether, into the physical body. When this at onement is performed you will find that not only is the physical body relaxed but also the spiritual body, the two are in unison and that is when good healing powers flow.

Always remember that when you have been given this gift, and developed it, you will begin to understand from whence this power comes. How the power reacts with people, then you will find that this gift is not only healing the patient but is also giving healing to yourself. So that is one way of healing oneself, by giving healing to others. Of course if one would attempt to heal oneself by oneself then there is only one way that this can be done, and you will find that this is in the physical sense of the word. For if I were to place my hand upon my other hand, were it sick, then I am using the same energy field, the same powers, whereas I need to have an energy field of someone else. But one can heal oneself through correct breathing and relaxation. Of course, I can understand my body more and eliminate poisons or substances that have come from the body, by eating properly and taking note of when the elementary tract is performed. You will find that there are certain nature calls that happen within your body. Never reject these but act almost immediately upon them and always drink your quota of water for the oxygen that is needed. Healing is the subject that not only goes back thousands of years but it is an art that has been performed not only by intellectuals, or so-called intellectuals, but has been performed by people who had not the scientific knowledge that you have today but at the same time inherent within them was the same healing energy that you also have.

Christ was one of these healers. I'm taking Christ as one of these healers because all of you know of and about Christ. You will find that most of the spiritual leaders of that time were those that performed healing. You will find that this performance of one man trying to better another mans life by healing is the format for the betterment of mankind. You will find that most of those spiritual leaders of that time did healing, if not by physical means, by spiritual means, even so as your latter day Spiritualists.

There are those that require healing that cannot receive healing, simply because there is a mental barrier they set up within their own conscious state that simply rejects any form of healing whatsoever. There are those that are receptive even to the ether, these people receive healing because their own psychic channels are open, they are ones who do not waste their energy. They might not perform healing by our standard but they send out their energy into the ether to those people that are on their beds of sickness, or even to those who are poor in spirit. In other words they send out this energy so that it can be garnered from the ether by others who are receptive and able to receive it or take it from the ether. There are those who are healed simply by faith; you all remember the woman who had an issue of blood for about six months and she touched the hem of Christ's garment. Christ knew that she had touched his garment because he could sense her aura, her energy field which had merged with Christ's own energy field or Bio-Plasmic power. That is how Christ was able to sense her touch, and He turned to this woman saying, "Thy Faith has made thee whole," and she was then without issue of blood.

Christ, many of you might know, whose healing ministry was just about three years old, was brought up in the Galilean knowledge of an ethnic group within the Palestinians, the Essenes and these were a strict neo religious group who practiced the art of healing.

There is no doubt that Christ was indoctrinated into this art of healing but let not that take anything away from Christ with his remarkable healing powers, healing in fact of the highest order. There has been as high at times but never so frequent as Christ's. This is because there was the perfect unison between Christ and the Creator, between Christ and God, between Christ and Spirit, between Christ and the Cosmic Power or Force of the Creator of Life. A cosmic force that is open to each and every one of you with designs to lay his hands upon another person to heal. Or who desires to be able to project their creative thoughts, their positive thoughts, out to those who are on beds of sickness, so that that thought-energy may travel to that patient and be used by those from spirit who are also using their own powers, this cosmic force.

What does one mean by cosmic force; you all know that a human body is made up of earth, air, fire and water. Well all of these things come from the Sun and the Sun is just a small, tiny part of the Cosmos within our own small Planetary or Solar System. This cosmic power, this power from the Sun, will grow food in the ground, will nourish our bodies, will give us warmth, will give us light by day, and light by night with it's reflection from the Moon's surface. That is part of cosmic law,

The Sunshine Of My Life

a very tiny part indeed. But also remember that we are but like tiny grains of sand in a desert and in as much as we are part of that desert so we are part of God, part of cosmic law.

This cosmic law that man is trying to harness, this understanding of the Atomic structure, this could give man a great deal of healing for the physical body. This Atomic structure that could be of benefit to man untold, that is part of cosmic law. Everywhere in the universe is built up of atoms. Atoms which can be broken down by man's own doing or can be broken down by nature's own forces of cosmic law, by the Sun, which speeds towards this earthplane, sub-atomic particles such as Protons, Quarks and Tachyons. These are some of the make-up of particles of light that incorporate themselves into all living things. Some of them do their work upon the human body which might keep an equilibrium there, which might be needed to regenerate some parts, some damaged cells in the body. Protons are travelling right through your own body at this moment of time, and they keep on travelling through the very chair that you are sitting on, through the floor, indeed nothing is able to hold them. If one could harness the energy that there are in Protons then mankind would be able to orbit the whole of the universe, almost at the speed of light. When God created this earthplane, indeed the entire universe, he created the whole. I expect that it must have taken eons of time, by our own Earth standards, to create this source of energy. As you will remember, there was a void and within the void there was the voice of God, or in other words the energy of God, the energy that has always been there in the void because indeed this is cosmic energy. This is the energy I have been talking about which can destroy, or degenerate, or indeed it can regenerate. God tended to this cosmic energy, never forgetting that there is such a thing as Ecology. He made everything convertable so that it could be converted from energy to mass, because concentrated energy is mass, as you would discover if you

The Sunshine Of My Life

become a healer or even a member of a group of healers, who heal by thought. Concentrated thought is concentrated energy and that concentrated energy becomes mass. If one intended to give healing to one who had, for example, electric shocks to the head and part of the brain was damaged, then these parts that were damaged could be regenerated because God didn't make things that ecology would not touch. Even if your earthplane was devastated it would rise up again as it is today, this also applies to the human body.

When we are talking of outside influences, this outside energy, then of course we are talking about protons that flow through the body which I believe are inherent. As for the guides, or controls, or your spirit friends, the ones that you look to when you do your healing, even if your healing is by inspiration, don't forget where this help and inspiration comes from, it comes from spirit. There is a very high order of medicine within spirit that has come to the understanding that it is possible to direct this energy, this outside force and direct it to the seat of the trouble in a persons physical body. Even building flesh where there is no flesh, even a persons joints that have become calcified, swollen, possibly with arthritis, these can be broken down and rebuilt up as perfect, This is all done by cosmic law. Many healings are performed which even surprise the healers but when this healing does take place then there is a feeling of elation within the healer. With this elation comes the feeling of being priveledged, the feeling that spirit is encompassing them, a feeling of at onement with spirit and even a presumption to feel an at onement with God. But one must not get a sense of grandeur, one must not let the ego go travelling off at a tangent, one must not feel sublime, one must be humble. Because only some are chosen to heal, even though all of mankind has this healing inherent within them.

GOD BLESS YOU."